06/'08

Ghosts
and
Spirits

LEMONT PUBLIC LIBRARY DISTRICT
50 East Wend Street
Lemont, IL 60439-6439

SECRETS OF THE SUPERNATURAL

Ghosts and Spirits

REBECCA STEFOFF

Marshall Cavendish
Benchmark
New York

Marshall Cavendish Benchmark
99 White Plains Road
Tarrytown, New York 10591-9001
www.marshallcavendish.us

Library of Congress Cataloging-in-Publication Data
Stefoff, Rebecca
Ghosts / Rebecca Stefoff.
p. cm. — (Secrets of the supernatural)
Summary: "A critical exploration of ghosts and haunted houses"
—Provided by publisher.
Includes bibliographical references and index.
ISBN-13: 978-0-7614-2634-9
1. Ghosts. 2. Haunted houses. I. Title. II. Series.
BF1461.S82 2007
133.1—dc22
2006031652

Editor: Joyce Stanton
Publisher: Michelle Bisson
Editorial Director: Michelle Bisson
Art Director: Anahid Hamparian
Series Designer: Anne Scatto / PIXEL PRESS

Images provided by Rose Corbett Gordon, Art Editor, Mystic CT, from the following sources:
Cover: The Art Archive/Musée des Beaux Arts Besançon/Dagli Orti; *Back cover:* Getty Images; *Page 1:* L'Oratorio
dei Disciplini Clusone, Bergamo, Italy/SuperStock; *page 2:* Erich Lessing/Art Resource, NY; *page 6:* ArenaPal/
Topham/The Image Works; *pages 9, 36, 37, 40, 42:* Haunted Museum Library; *pages 12, 19, 43, 58, 67:* Mary Evans
Picture Library/The Image Works; *pages 14, 17, 53:* Getty Images; *page 16:* Owaki/Kulla/Corbis; *page 21:* Jeffrey
Allan Salter/Corbis; *page 22:* Adoc-photos/Art Resource, NY; *page 24:* The Art Archive/Dagli Orti (A); *page 25:*
Church of San Francesco, Assisi, Italy/SuperStock; *page 27:* Richard T. Nowitz/Corbis; *page 30:* The Art Archive/
Pinacoteca Repossi Chiari Brescia/Dagli Orti (A); *page 32:* David Samuel Robbins/Corbis; *page 33:* Gideon
Mendel/Corbis; *pages 35, 61, 68:* The Granger Collection, NY; *page 38:* Snark/Art Resource, NY; *page 45:* Charles
Walker/Topfoto/The Image Works; *page 47:* San Diego Historical Society Research Library & Photograph
Archives; *page 51:* Private Collection/© Gavin Graham Gallery, London, UK/The Bridgeman Art Library;
pages 54, 56, 59, 62: Hulton Archive/Getty Images; *page 64:* The Art Archive/Culver Pictures; *page 70:* Liz Hafalla/
San Francisco Chronicle/Corbis; *page 72:* Dana Spaeth/SuperStock; *page 75:* Jessica Rinaldi/Reuters/Corbis; *page
78:* Time & Life Pictures/Getty Images; *page 80:* Christoph Wilhelm/Getty Images; *page 83:* Robert Place.

Printed in Malaysia

1   3   5   6   4   2

FRONT COVER: This haunting figure appears in the work of
   nineteenth-century French painter Gustave Courbet.
BACK COVER: A haunted house?
HALF TITLE: The dance of death, painted in Italy in the fifteenth
   century, a time when terrible plagues turned people's thoughts
   to death and ghosts.
TITLE PAGE: A shrieking specter from a Japanese ghost story
   bears the severed head of her victim.

Contents

Some houses seem to take on a life all their own—
or maybe not their own. . . .

Is It True?

Late at night the children heard a noise like something chewing on the wooden posts of their bed. The boy and girl pulled the blanket over their heads.

"Rats," whispered six-year-old Richard Bell. "It's rats!"

His older sister, Betsy, shivered. "No," she said. "It's worse than rats."

Richard felt Betsy grab his hand. "Do you hear it?" she said softly into his ear.

"What do you hear, Betsy?" Richard clung to his big sister, trying not to cry.

"The voice," she answered. "Someone's tryin' to talk to us, far, far away."

Suddenly the blanket flew off the bed. Richard screamed as his pillow was yanked from beneath his head by invisible hands.

That was the beginning of the Bell family's nightmare. The year was 1817. The place was Robertson County, Tennessee, where the town of Adams now stands.

The children heard frightening sounds almost every night.

Blankets and pillows were thrown from their bed. Betsy Bell's hair was pulled, but nobody was seen pulling it. Someone slapped her—someone invisible! Soon the invisible hands started slapping and pinching other people, and sticking them with needles.

By all accounts, John Bell's family was haunted. Some say, though, that when he died, the hauntings stopped.

Before long, friends and neighbors were talking about the haunting of the Bell family. The mysterious voice got louder. Some people said it sounded like an old woman singing, or praying. Others said the ghost was cursing. Only a witch would be wicked enough to curse like that—it must be the spirit of a witch! The story spread to Nashville, where it came to the ears of General Andrew Jackson, the hero of the Battle of New Orleans in the War of 1812.

Richard and Betsy's father, John Bell, had been one of Jackson's soldiers. When Jackson heard about the haunting, he decided to see for himself what was going on. The story goes that Jackson spent one night on the Bell farm and then left, saying, "I'd rather fight the British again than have any more dealings with that torment."

The Bells' troubles went on until John Bell fell sick and died. Some stories about the haunting say that the witch hated John and had sworn to kill him. Some even say that she poisoned him, and when he died, her long, shrill laugh echoed through the house. . . .

The Bell Witch legend has been called "America's Greatest Ghost Story." It was the source of several recent books and the 2005 movie *An American Haunting*. The state of Tennessee even put up a roadside sign near the spot where it is said the haunting happened.

But, despite all the publicity, a big question about the story remains: Is it true?

That question is part of an even larger one: Do ghosts exist?

Out of This World

Ghosts and spirits are dead people who can make themselves known to the living. They are called supernatural and paranormal because they are

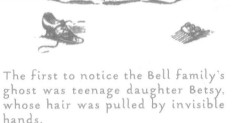

The first to notice the Bell family's ghost was teenage daughter Betsy, whose hair was pulled by invisible hands.

"beyond nature" and "outside what is normal." Ghosts and spirits can't be explained by science—at least, not by today's scientific knowledge. (Remember, people thought electricity was mysterious, or even magical, before science advanced far enough to explain it.)

Some people are very sure that ghosts exist. Others are just as sure that there's no such thing as ghosts. But no one has ever been able to prove beyond doubt that ghosts are real *or* imaginary. The best anyone can do is show *why* they think what they think.

People who say that they've seen ghosts are claiming that something outside the ordinary happened to them. Think about what that means.

Suppose a friend told you, "I saw a movie star on the street this morning!" That seems pretty special. After all, unless you live in Hollywood, you don't see movie stars every day. But you know that people *do* see movie stars walking around in real life. Maybe you've seen one yourself. So you know that your friend's claim is not impossible. You check the newspaper or the Internet and learn that the movie star is in your town making a film. Do you know for certain that your friend saw the star this morning? That depends upon whether you think your friend is honest. If you can't think of any reason not to trust your friend, you'll probably accept the claim as true.

Would you feel the same if your friend said, "I saw a ghost last night"?

Seeing a ghost is a lot more out of the ordinary than seeing a movie star—and a lot harder to prove.

People who study the paranormal sometimes say, "Extraordinary claims require extraordinary proof." This means that the more unusual a claim is, the stronger the evidence must be. Your friend's word about seeing a movie star is not very strong proof, but you might accept it anyway, because the claim could easily be true. To believe that your friend saw a ghost, you might want stronger proof, because the claim is extraordinary.

People who ask for extraordinarily solid proof before they believe extraordinary things are called skeptics. A skeptic doesn't say that there's no truth to the supernatural or paranormal. A skeptic just says, "Show me proof that the occurrence can't be explained by natural, normal means."

Do you want to know the truth about ghosts, whatever it might be? Unfortunately, it isn't always possible to find the truth, especially in the case of old stories. You might have to decide what is *most likely* to be true. One useful tool is critical thinking, a way of using reason and asking questions to get at the truth. Critical thinking means taking a careful look at the things people say—especially the extraordinary things—and checking the evidence.

Thinking for Yourself

Let's say you see a photograph of a mysterious glowing shape. The photographer says it's a ghost, caught on camera! But if you have some experience with photography, or if you do a little research, you may know that lots of spooky-looking pictures have been created by natural means.

A photographer can take one picture of an empty staircase and another picture of a person. If those two images are superimposed (overlaid on the same piece of film, or blended in a computer), a ghostly figure can seem to be floating down the stairs. Or light can leak into a camera body, putting unexpected blurs or streaks of light into the picture. Such things can happen by mistake, or they can be done on purpose, to make trick photos.

So what about that picture you're examining? A skeptic would say that the photo is not enough to prove that ghosts exist, because it *could* have been created by natural means.

But you should also remember another saying from paranormal research: "Absence of evidence does not mean evidence of absence." This twisty-sounding saying has a simple meaning. If a piece of evi-

A "spirit photograph" made in 1910. The photographer made a picture of someone dressed as a ghost, then used a slide prepared with the "ghost" image to photograph the man sitting at the desk.

dence fails to prove that ghosts exist, that doesn't mean that ghosts *don't exist*. Even if *every* piece of ghost evidence ever collected is worthless, ghosts might exist—they're just not proven.

To decide for yourself what to think about ghosts and spirits, you'll have to act like a juror at a trial. Listen to the arguments on both sides of the case. Look closely at the evidence, because you want your decision to be based on facts. But keep an open mind. Be willing to look at new evidence, even if it doesn't fit the ideas you already have.

In the pages that follow, you'll hear from people who've seen ghosts, and you'll explore some of the world's most haunted places. You'll watch investigators find natural explanations for some spooky phenomena, or happenings. And you'll find more information about the Bell Witch, so you can make up your own mind about "America's Greatest Ghost Story."

Ghosts don't have to be human. Many people claim to have seen ghostly animals. In one modern case, a girl saw visions of a large, dark shape and also a small dog.

Ghosts Among Us

When heavy footsteps crossed a room upstairs, the woman who lived in the house thought someone had broken into her home. She tried to send her dog up to frighten the intruder, but the dog wouldn't go up the stairs. Finally, the woman went up—and no one was there.

That was the first strange thing that happened after a woman named Shelley and her daughter moved into an old house in Halifax, England. But it wasn't the last. The footsteps came back a few nights later. Shelley also heard a "snoring" sound and "loud dragging noises."

The kitchen of the house was especially eerie. Once when Shelley was in the kitchen, an invisible hand threw a coin at her. Another time, something seemed to stroke her arm. But the worst thing was the time that Shelley was using a mixing bowl, and something tapped on it. She asked out loud if there was someone there. For answer she received many loud, quick taps.

Two days later, fire destroyed the kitchen. Fortunately, Shelley and her daughter were away at the time. Since then, the kitchen has been rebuilt, and nothing strange has happened in it. But Shelley's daughter has seen visions of a small dog and a large, dark shape like a man.

"A white mist drifting up the path towards my front door" frightened a woman who thought her house was haunted. Mist like this might easily make someone think of ghosts.

"I have also seen a white mist drifting up the path towards my front door," Shelley wrote on a paranormal Web site, "and my dog has taken to sitting and staring at the door as though waiting for something to come in. I hope it never does!!"

Shelley claimed that her story was true. She is one of thousands of people who say they have had firsthand experience with ghosts. But Shelley's story also shows how hard it is to get at the truth about ghosts. She may have made up all of the details for fun, just as if she were writing a ghost story. Or she may genuinely think that the things she wrote about really happened, even though she imagined them.

Or she and her daughter may have been visited by ghosts.

Everyone has read ghost stories. Libraries are full of scary tales of spooks, spirits, specters, apparitions, and phantoms—all names for ghosts. But there is a difference between stories that are written as fiction and stories like Shelley's, which the teller claims to be true. "True ghost stories" are sometimes called ghost reports, ghost claims, or ghost accounts.

In scientific studies, a person who sees or hears a ghost is called a percipient—a fancy word for "one who perceives, or sees." In

Shelley's story, she was the percipient. Over the years, percipients have included doctors, scientists, and judges. But whether they are professionals trained to observe and use their powers of reason, or ordinary people like Shelley, percipients have one thing in common: their reports are anecdotes.

An anecdote is a story. It is not backed up by other kinds of proof, such as photographs, recordings, or physical evidence. It may be supported by statements from other witnesses—but these are anecdotes, too. Most anecdotes don't have many details that an outside investigator can check. An anecdote about something that happened to *someone else* is even less solid. Stories based on words like "and then he said" or "she told me" are called hearsay. In court, they do not count as evidence.

With an anecdote, all you can do is take the story-teller's word—or not. We all know that people make

An eerie spectral presence? Or just a light reflected in a window?

things up from time to time, for fun or to get attention. So a percipient could be lying. But there is another explanation.

Psychology, the science of the mind, has shown that we can't always trust our senses. It's not unusual for people to see and hear things that aren't really there, especially at night, when many ghost sightings happen. When it's dark, and people are tired, ordinary sights and sounds can turn into something else in the mind. A person who claims to have seen a ghost could be honest, but mistaken.

Maybe Shelley's experiences really happened, but they can be explained in ways that aren't supernatural. The feeling of being stroked on the arm, for example, might have been caused by a draft of air moving through the kitchen. That feeling can also be caused by a natural event called piloerection. It happens to people and many kinds of animals, if they are cold, startled, or worried. Piloerection means that the hairs bristle, or stand up, on the back of the neck, the arms, or the back. It can seem like a light touch, or it can make us say things like "my hair stood on end" or "my spine tingled." If your hair stood up like that, even for a natural reason, you might think there was a ghost nearby!

When critical thinkers hear ghost reports, they ask: What is the source of the information? Is it reliable? Can the evidence be checked? Can the mysterious phenomena be explained by natural means? Are there any reasons why the percipient might have imagined seeing a ghost? When it's not possible to prove a claim true *or* false, a critical thinker is not afraid to say, "I don't know."

All in the Mind?

Shelley's story of noises and a thrown coin is a lot like reports of poltergeists. A poltergeist is a type of disturbance that often happens around young people, especially girls. Its name comes from

A poltergeist, or "knocking spirit," creates a disturbance by throwing chairs through the air and knocking pictures from the wall.

the German words for "knocking spirit." Poltergeist cases usually involve strange noises and moving objects, but not ghosts that can be seen.

One well-known poltergeist case happened in 1960. It involved an eleven-year-old girl named Virginia who lived with relatives in Scotland. Virginia's doctor and teacher said that she was healthy and above average in intelligence.

The disturbances started with a "thunking" sound that followed Virginia around the house. It ended when she fell asleep. The next day, a piece of heavy furniture near Virginia suddenly moved five inches. The family brought in witnesses, including Virginia's teacher, two doctors, and a minister. They heard knocking sounds coming from Virginia's bed or from the air near her. Furniture near Virginia sometimes moved without anyone touching it, at home and at school. The noises followed Virginia when she visited relatives in another town. After a couple of weeks, the disturbances stopped.

Cases like Virginia's are not rare. People used to think they were caused by elves, goblins, or some kind of mischievous or evil spirit. Today, many ghost researchers think that poltergeist activity comes from the living, not from spirits. But they don't agree on the cause.

Some paranormal researchers think that poltergeist activity is caused by an unknown form of energy created by the thoughts or emotions of the person at the center of the phenomena. It is powerful enough to move objects and create noises. Researchers have coined the term psychokinetic (from the Greek words for "moving by mind") energy to describe this force. They sometimes call it PK. But they have not yet been able to measure PK, or even prove that it exists.

If psychokinetic energy exists, could it be caused by strong feelings, or by the physical and emotional changes of young people who are growing up? Maybe this mysterious energy is responsible for poltergeist activity, and the people who cause the disturbances aren't doing it on purpose. But some poltergeist activity has been shown to be trickery.

In 1984, a fourteen-year-old girl named Tina Resch lived in Columbus, Ohio. Strange things started happening in her house. Telephones flew across the room. Lamps crashed to the floor. After newspapers reported the poltergeist disturbance, a professional magician named James Randi looked into the case.

Randi is one of a long line of skilled illusionists who have investigated paranormal claims. Good magicians are experts at fooling people. Without supernatural help, they create many of the same eerie effects that happen in hauntings and poltergeist cases. Often, they can show how someone else is fooling people, too. But the Tina Resch case didn't need Randi's special skills. A television crew's video camera was left on by accident, and Tina got caught pulling over a lamp when she thought no one could see her.

Poltergeist cases occur all over the world. Ghost believers, scientists, and skeptics study these strange disturbances, hoping to discover just what causes them. But to most people, the word *ghost* means something more disturbing than a loud thump or a knocking sound. It means a visitor from beyond the grave.

Professional magician James Randi promotes critical thinking about the supernatural. His educational foundation offers a million dollars for proof of a supernatural or paranormal event or power. The prize has never been claimed.

A photo from the 1860s shows French magician Henri Robin with a spooky, sheet-clad skeleton. This type of ghost resembles the risen dead, but ghosts are also described as balls of light, or vapors, or ordinary people.

A History of Hauntings

I n William Shakespeare's play *Hamlet,* the character Horatio tells of strange omens that appeared in ancient Rome before the death of its famous ruler Julius Caesar. Graves were found empty, and "the sheeted dead / Did squeak and gibber in the Roman streets."

Why "sheeted dead"? For centuries, bodies were wrapped in sheets, or long pieces of cloth called shrouds, before they were buried. People thought that if the spirits of the dead rose from the grave, they would be wearing these burial shrouds. The sheet-draped figure became part of ghost lore, but ghosts have taken a vast variety of forms.

Changing Ideas about Ghosts

People have been seeing spirits since the dawn of history. Some of the oldest writings in the world come from cities in the ancient Middle East five thousand years ago. They tell of restless ghosts who tormented the living by chasing them in the streets, appearing in their houses, and haunting their dreams. These angry ghosts were the spirits of people who had died young or by violence, and felt cheated out of their lives.

To the ancient Greeks and Romans, ghosts often appeared draped in their burial shrouds.

By about twenty-five centuries ago, the Greeks had a different view of ghosts. Two ancient Greek epics called the *Iliad* and the *Odyssey*—long poems about war, adventure, and the deeds of gods and heroes—say that when warriors died on the battlefield, their ghosts left their bodies and flew, squeaking like bats, down to an underworld called Hades.

Greek ghosts weren't very frightening, and they never left the underworld. They stood in Hades forever, talking to each other in low voices about their family histories and the great battles they had fought. This afterlife was so boring that one ghost moaned, "I would rather be a servant in a poor man's house and be above ground than be king of kings among the dead."

But a few centuries later, the spirits of the dead were once again making trouble for the living. The ancient Romans believed in several kinds of ghosts. The most common were lemures, spirits of dead relatives or ancestors. Lemures haunted their families and descendants, especially during the month of May. The Romans held special ceremonies and festivals to drive them away. Drums were used for ghost busting because the lemures hated loud noises.

The Roman writer Pliny the Younger wrote about a ghost that haunted a house in the Greek city of Athens. At night a spirit appeared in the house. It looked like a scruffy old man with chains on his arms and legs. He rattled his chains and beckoned to the frightened people of the house, who ran away. Then a learned man named Athenodorus rented the house. When the ghost appeared, Athenodorus didn't run. Instead, he followed the ghost into the garden. The ghost suddenly vanished. The next day Athenodorus dug a hole at the spot where it had disappeared. He found a skeleton in chains. After he took off the chains and gave the skeleton a proper burial, the ghost was never seen again.

During the Middle Ages, ghosts became even scarier. In Christian

Christians in medieval Europe feared that ghosts were associated with the devil or with evil beings such as these flying demons.

Europe, most people believed that the souls of the virtuous dead went to heaven while those of sinners went to hell. A spirit that appeared to the living had to be sent by either God or the devil.

The devil used the ghosts of sinners to tempt living people to sin. God used sinners' ghosts, too, but as warnings. If a girl had sinned by dancing too much in life, or perhaps dancing in a churchyard, her ghost appeared whirling and spinning in agony. Her punishment was a warning to other girls not to dance. Or a man who had stolen a pair of shoes might come back as a blood-dripping ghost whose feet had been chopped off—a sign of the dreadful fate that awaited thieves.

Sounds and Sights of Spooks

Ghosts' voices have changed over the years, says Ronald C. Finucane, a historian who has studied ghost reports from many centuries. In ancient times, ghosts squeaked like bats or murmured in faint voices. During the Middle Ages, they spoke in deep, echoing voices. Later, ghosts spoke more normally, but around the nineteenth century they fell silent. Apparitions in most ghost stories and reports from the nineteenth and early twentieth centuries made no sounds. Today, specters sometimes speak again, often in whispers.

The way ghosts look has changed, too. To the ancient people of Mesopotamia, now known as Iraq, ghosts could take three forms. One looked like a living person, one was a walking skeleton, and one was a ferocious monster, often with the head of an animal such as a bull.

Greek and Roman ghosts had human form. They appeared naked, or dressed in the clothes they had worn in life, or draped in rags or sheets. Ghosts of the Middle Ages often wore white sheets, but they could also be covered with fire, dripping with blood, or carrying their own heads as punishment for the sins they had committed in life.

Later, ghosts became more solid and ordinary-looking. Then, in the nineteenth century, they became filmy and faint. They walked through walls or melted into clouds of mist. Sometimes they were invisible.

Modern ghosts may be getting solid again. Many ghost reports now have spirits dressed like ordinary people. Sometimes a percipient sees an unknown person or child and doesn't even know it's a ghost until it vanishes into thin air.

If ghosts really exist, shouldn't they look the same in all times and places? Maybe not. Some ghost believers feel that there are many kinds of ghosts. They

During the nineteenth century, ghosts were usually said to be filmy and transparent. Many ghost reports included the words "I could see right through it!"

also think that spirits can wear different things. Some wear whatever they were buried in, while others wear outfits they loved in life. Or spirits can take the form of pure energy, appearing as balls or waves of light.

Another explanation comes from psychology. Experiments have shown that our minds often "read" the world around us based on what we expect. If you've read a lot of ghost stories, or seen a lot of TV shows and movies about ghosts, you are "primed" with information about ghosts. The next time you see or hear something you don't understand, you might be more likely to think it is a ghost than if you had never read or talked about ghosts. And if you do see a ghost, it probably won't be an old-fashioned specter, wearing a sheet and rattling chains. It will most likely resemble something from a modern spooky movie, such as *The Sixth Sense,* or a TV show.

Ghosts and the Media

The media may be making people believe in ghosts. That's what Glenn Sparks, a communication professor at Purdue University in Indiana, discovered when he surveyed 120 people about their belief in the supernatural and paranormal—and their TV habits.

One of the main reasons for belief in the supernatural or paranormal, Sparks learned, is personal experience. Some of the people he surveyed were believers because they had experienced something out of the ordinary, or thought they had. But what about believers who didn't have personal experiences? What makes someone who has never seen a ghost believe in ghosts?

Age, family background, religion, and education all influence whether or not someone believes in the paranormal without experiencing it, Sparks says. But, he adds, "Television may explain 10 percent of the belief in the paranormal." Sparks found that people who watched TV shows about supernatural subjects were more likely to believe in the supernatural than people who didn't watch such shows. This was true whether the shows were fictional stories, such as *The X-Files,* or ones that claimed to present facts, such as *Unsolved Mysteries.* Both kinds of shows pushed people toward believing. When it comes to ghosts, it seems, it's always hard to tell fact from fiction.

Some accounts of spectral visitations say that ghosts visit
the living for a reason, as when a dead woman's spirit returns to
comfort her grieving husband. Sometimes, though, the ghost's
business with the living is more sinister. . . .

What Do Ghosts Want?

I f ghosts do roam the world of the living, what is it that they want? Are they evil beings who want to harm the living? Are they sad, lost souls, trying desperately to communicate with us? Or are they kind, compassionate spirits who want to help us?

"Most ghosts are totally neutral and mean no harm," says Richard Senate, author of several books about spirits. Sometimes, ghosts even do good deeds. Kirsten, a young woman from Oxford, Michigan, was six years old when she saw a woman's face materialize in her room. After that, she saw the woman's ghost from time to time. She lost her fear of it, and even became fond of it. Then, one night when Kirsten was sixteen, the ghost woke her up and led her to the hallway, where Kirsten saw smoke coming from her brother's room. Kirsten put out the fire with an extinguisher. She never saw the ghost again, although she believes that it saved her life.

Good Ghosts and Bad

Some cultures see spirits as forces of good. They are ancestors who have gone to the afterlife but continue to protect their families or

A mourner at a Chinese cemetery spreads a banquet in honor of dead ancestors.

communities. China, Mexico, and some other parts of the world have rituals in which the living honor the dead, usually by bringing food or gifts to graves on special days. People in these cultures believe, however, that if they forget to honor the dead, the ghosts will come back and cause trouble.

The Malagasy people of Madagascar, a large island off the coast of Africa, say that unhappy spirits can turn into dangerous ghosts called *angatra.* So the Malagasy try to keep the spirits happy. At rituals called bone-turnings, they dig up their ancestors and wrap the bones in clean new shrouds. Because ghosts like quiet, the Malagasy don't make loud noises near graves.

Another restless, unhappy spirit is the duppy, from the Caribbean island of Jamaica. Duppies are eager to harm the living. A person can send duppies after his enemy if he is willing to pay them (their

Wrapped anew in fresh white cloths, dead people dug up from a cemetery in Madagascar are paraded before being returned to the ground.

favorite payment is the alcoholic drink rum). To avoid angering these troublesome ghosts, you're never supposed to throw water without first warning duppies to get out of the way.

Ghosts sometimes seem to be social "police," trying to make people act right and follow society's rules. A woman whose husband has died might be haunted by his ghost if she got married again too soon. A man who got money from his dead parents might be haunted by their spirits if he didn't share the money with his brothers and sisters. With ghost reports like these, especially if they are from long ago, it's hard to tell which came first—the bad behavior or the ghost. One possible explanation is that a person who secretly feels guilty about something imagines seeing a ghost. The ghost is like a guilty conscience. Another explanation is that people need to feel there is *a reason* for hauntings. If someone starts having ghost trouble, the community looks for a reason.

Remember the Bell Witch haunting from the beginning of this book? After John Bell died and the haunting ended, people said that the "witch" who had troubled his family was the spirit of an old neighbor woman named Kate, who thought John had cheated her out of some property. This made it easier for people to understand why the Bells had suffered.

Messengers of Death

Like Pliny's story about the ragged ghost in Athens, many ghost reports end in the discovery of an improperly buried skeleton. A common theme of ghost reports around the world is the spirit seeking burial, or calling attention to its unmarked grave.

Another common theme—the ghost who warns of death—appeared during the Middle Ages, when whole nations lived in fear of sudden death from barbarian attacks or the plague. Pope Gregory the Great, who died in 604, wrote about a monk named John who went to the cemetery after a friend died. Later, John told the other monks that he had heard the dead man's voice calling to him from the grave. John was sure it was a warning of his own death—and ten days later he died.

In 1917, during World War I, a young English woman was living in India. Her brother was a military pilot. One day she was startled to see him in her living room. She thought he had come for a surprise visit—until he disappeared! Later she learned that just when she saw the vision, her brother's plane was shot down in combat over France.

A famous poet once saw an apparition of his wife. John Donne was a poet and church official in London in the early seventeenth century. When he was asked to go with other men to Paris on the king's business, his pregnant wife begged him not to go. But

Donne felt he must go, so he made the twenty-day journey. Two days after the men reached Paris, one of them found Donne terribly upset. "I have seen a dreadful vision," Donne said. "I have seen my dear wife pass twice through this room, with her hair hanging about her shoulders and a dead child in her arms." Donne's friend told him it was only a dream, but Donne was sure it was real. Soon afterward, a messenger from London reported that Donne's wife was very ill. At the time he saw her appear in Paris, she gave birth to their child, who was born dead.

Avenging Spirits

Avenging spirits haunt the living for a special purpose—to get even with those who harmed them. Take the case of the Greenbrier Ghost of West Virginia.

In 1896, when Zona Heaster was about twenty-two years old, she married Edward Shue. He was a newcomer in her hometown of Greenbrier. They hadn't known each other long. And they weren't

Zona Heaster Shue was said to have appeared as a ghost after her death—to reveal who killed her.

married for long. By January of 1897, Zona was dead.

Edward Shue was at work when an errand boy found the stiff, cold body of the young bride on the floor of her kitchen. When Edward heard the tragic news, he ran home. A doctor arrived and decided that Zona had died of heart failure. She was buried soon afterward.

Zona's mother, Mary Heaster, was grief-stricken. But she was also suspicious. She had never liked Zona's husband, and she felt that there was something strange about her daughter's sudden death. Then, one night, Zona appeared in Mary Heaster's room. When Mary reached out to touch her daughter, Zona vanished.

But a few days later she appeared again, and this time she told her mother how she had died. Her husband had flown into a rage because she hadn't cooked any meat for his supper. He had grabbed her throat and broken her neck!

Mary Heaster told relatives and friends about the visits from Zona's ghost. Many of them thought grief had caused Mary to imagine the ghost. Eventually, though, her brother-in-law agreed that the matter should be investigated. They told Mary's story to an officer of the court, who ordered Zona's body to be dug up and examined. The court officer also looked into Edward Shue's background and found that he had been married twice before. Each of his wives had died in a strange accident. One of them had died of a broken neck.

The doctor reexamined Zona's corpse and admitted that he might have been wrong about the cause of death. Then he discovered that one of her neck bones was broken. Edward Shue was tried for murder, found guilty, and sent to prison, where he died in 1905.

Zona Heaster Shue has been called "The Ghost That Solved Its Own Murder." One Web page about the story says, "In one of the most remarkable cases on U.S. court records, Zona Heaster Shue *did* speak from her grave, revealing not only how she died—but

at whose hand. Her ghost's testimony not only named her own murderer, but helped in convicting the culprit in a court of law. It is the only case on U.S. lawbooks in which the testimony from the spirit of a murder victim aided in resolving the crime."

The Greenbrier case looks like a perfect example of an avenging ghost—a murdered woman whose spirit came back from the grave to see that justice was done. And that might be exactly what happened. But what do we really know about the case?

First, Zona died. Second, Zona's

Mary Heaster's stubborn insistence that she had seen her daughter's ghost finally led West Virgina officials to investigate Zona's death.

mother claimed that Zona's ghost had appeared and told how she died. Third, Zona's mother and another relative got the court to take a closer look at the case. (It's not unusual for a court to order a body to be dug up and reexamined if foul play is suspected.) Fourth, examination of Zona's body showed that she died from a broken neck. Fifth, her husband was convicted of murdering her.

Zona's ghost did not testify in court against her murderer. Mary Heaster testified that she had seen Zona's ghost, but no one else ever claimed to see or hear the ghost. Edward Shue was convicted of murder on the evidence of a broken neck bone, not on ghostly testimony. Yet how could Mary Heaster have known about the neck bone if Zona's ghost hadn't told her? Are there any other possible explanations?

Did the ghost of a murdered woman return to demand justice? There is no proof of such a thing, but some ghost believers think that "unfinished business" can call a spirit back from the realm of the dead.

Some versions of the Greenbrier story say that Edward dressed his wife's corpse himself and would not let anyone handle Zona's head before she was buried. Maybe this made Mary wonder about Zona's neck. Maybe Mary heard gossip about Edward Shue's earlier wives and their suspicious deaths. Maybe she made up the ghost story so that people would take her worries seriously. Or maybe Mary was so sad and upset that she imagined she saw her daughter's ghost.

Perhaps Zona really did speak to her mother from beyond the grave. We can never know. Mary Heaster's anecdote is not proof—even if it did go to court.

Borley Rectory has been called "the most haunted
house in England," or even in the world. The mysterious events that
took place there over the course of seven decades
and three different owners are still being debated today.

Spectral Sites

D o violent deaths leave an invisible mark on the places where
they happen? Are ghosts tied to the spots where they died,
or where their bones lie? Maybe that explains why certain places
have a reputation for being haunted. Strange things happen in these
places. People see eerie sights or hear mysterious sounds. Sometimes the hauntings go on for years, or even centuries.

The Most Famous Haunted House in History

Skeptics and ghost believers are still arguing about events in what
some people consider the world's best-known and most-investigated
haunting. Borley Rectory was a large brick house built in 1863 in the
English town of Borley by a rector, or church official, named Henry
Bull. He was the first to live in the house, along with his wife and,
eventually, fourteen children. But did something else dwell in Borley
Rectory, too?

Some members of the Bull family thought so. People said that
the ghost of a nun roamed the grounds and peered into windows.
Several of Bull's daughters saw her. Later, a phantom carriage

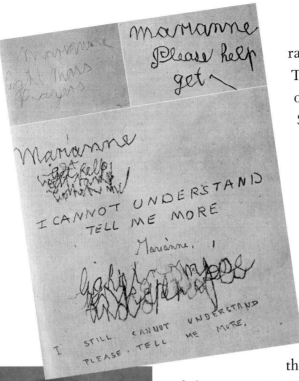

raced up the drive. The house was full of other mysteries, too. Strange sounds were heard. Books and lamps moved when no one was in the room. The smell of violets filled the air—in winter, when violets could not have been blooming.

Marianne Foyster reported being attacked by the Borley Rectory ghost, which also scrawled messages to her on the walls.

The last of the Bulls moved out of the rectory in 1927. The next people to live in the house, the Smiths, heard rumors that it was haunted. But the most terrifying events in Borley Rectory happened during the 1930s, when Lionel and Marianne Foyster and their adopted daughter lived in the house. Marianne Foyster reported being slapped and almost smothered by invisible hands. Bells rang, bottles were hurled across rooms, stones flew through windows, and messages to Marianne appeared scrawled on the walls.

Harry Price, a British paranormal investigator, visited Borley Rectory while the Smiths and then the Foysters lived there. Later he directed a year-long study of the house with a team of volunteers. By that time, Price was well known as a psychic detective and ghost hunter. Although he had exposed several fake mediums, he believed that some paranormal events were real.

Borley Rectory, Price declared in several books on the subject, was haunted. He claimed to have heard ghostly sounds, such as rapping noises and bells ringing in the house. Marks in the dust showed that candlesticks and other objects had been moved while rooms were empty.

Members of Price's team tried to communicate with the ghost in séances. They used a planchette, a device that lets a spirit spell out

A planchette glides across a board to spell out words. The device is supposedly moved by ghosts or spirits, but in this 1910 photo a girl shows how "spirit writing" can be faked, even when a person is blindfolded.

words. People at a séance place their hands on the planchette, and the spirit makes it glide across a paper or board marked with the alphabet (a critical thinker would ask whether it is really the spirit who is moving the planchette). In one séance at Borley, a murdered nun claimed to be the ghost—but later researchers have found no record of the nun. Then, on March 27, 1938, another séance brought a spirit warning that a fire in the hallway would destroy the house that night. Nothing happened.

Ever since Price's death in 1948, people have argued about his investigation of Borley Rectory. In 1956, another researcher reviewed Price's records of the case and decided that Price had faked the evidence for a haunting, maybe to sell his books. A second review said that the first review was full of mistakes, and that Price was an honest investigator. The argument about Harry Price goes on, but questions about Borley Rectory can never be answered. The building was destroyed due to damage in a fire that started in the hallway in February 1939.

Shaving a Spirit with Occam's Razor

Another English haunted house set ghost believers and skeptics arguing back in the early 1760s. A man named Parsons lived with his family in Cock Lane, in London. He rented an apartment in the house to a man named Kent and a woman named Fanny. Later, Kent moved out and sued Parsons over money. Around the same time, Fanny got sick and died.

Parsons started telling people that Kent had poisoned the woman and that her ghost haunted the house. The ghost communicated with Parsons's teenage daughter, Liz, through knocking sounds and scratches, usually while she was in bed. Parsons's claims became more and more amazing. Crowds came to the house to hear

Cock Lane,
circa 1760

the spirit knocking. Skeptics were sure that Liz was doing the "communicating," on her father's orders. When they found a piece of wood in her bed and showed that it could have been used to make the rapping sounds, Parsons went to jail for fraud. Yet many people continued to believe in the Cock Lane ghost.

The story of the Cock Lane ghost introduces a useful tool for critical thinking. The tool is a principle called Occam's razor, after a medieval thinker named William of Occam. It states that when you are faced with a number of possible explanations for something, you should choose the simplest one. In the case of the Cock Lane haunting, investigators found a girl and a stick. Those two things could explain the knocking sounds. There was no need to add a ghost.

Occam's razor slices through the confusion when you are weighing several possible explanations. It doesn't mean that the more complicated explanation is always wrong. It just means that if you can't prove the complicated explanation, you should stick with the simple one.

America's Most Haunted?

The United States has plenty of haunted houses. Quite a few of them even claim to be "America's Most Haunted House." But the Travel Channel's show *America's Most Haunted* gave the title to the Whaley House in San Diego, California. Over the years, the house has been a family home, a county courthouse, a theater, a ballroom, a billiard parlor, and more.

The first Whaley House ghost died horribly on the spot where the house now stands. In 1852, James Robinson was convicted of a serious crime in San Diego. The sentence was death. A wagon carried a gallows to an empty patch of ground. Local citizens gathered to watch the execution. The newspaper said that Robinson "kept his feet on the wagon as long as possible, but was finally pulled off. He swung back and forth like a pendulum until he strangled to death."

One of the watchers was Thomas Whaley. A few years later, he bought that patch of land and built a home for his family. *The San Diego Union* reported that "soon after the couple and their children moved in, heavy footsteps were heard moving about the house." Whaley thought they were made by the boots of a large man. He was sure it was Robinson's ghost.

Later, other ghosts began to haunt the unlucky house. Some visitors claim to have seen the ghosts of Thomas Whaley and

Thomas Whaley and his family were the first to live in a house built on a site where Whaley had witnessed a gruesome hanging.

his wife, wearing nineteenth-century clothes. A room that was once the courtroom seems to be haunted by the ghost of a small, dark-skinned woman wearing a long skirt and gold earrings. One ghost researcher claimed that he saw a phantom dog, probably a terrier, run down the hall with its ears flapping.

Today the Whaley House is California State Historic Landmark 65. It has been turned into a museum, and it is one of the most visited and studied haunted houses in the country. Still, no reliable proof of ghosts has come out of the Whaley House. Some of the sightings that have been reported over the years can be explained in nonghostly ways. In 1964, for example, television personality Regis Philbin thought he saw the spirit of Anna

Whaley on the wall of a darkened room in the house. "I got so excited I couldn't restrain myself!" he said. "I flipped on the light—and nothing was there but a portrait of Anna Whaley, the long-dead mistress of the house."

Investigating a Haunting

Regis Philbin's experience in the Whaley House shows that some spooky happenings in haunted houses have simple explanations. But most people find it hard to think about simple explanations once they have been startled by something they don't understand. Once the idea of a ghost gets into your mind, *everything* starts to look like ghost activity. Joe Nickell knows that.

Nickell is a researcher for the Committee for the Scientific Investigation of Claims of the Paranormal (CSICOP). One of his cases involved a haunted house in Virginia. A couple named George and Mary had moved into the house with their five pets. As soon as they moved in, they heard some strange stories. A neighbor told them that someone had been shot in the house, and that a little boy had died there. One night George and Mary saw a large bright light move across their kitchen, and a door slammed by itself. Mary started to think the house was haunted.

A few months later, Mary was in her bedroom when she heard a child giggling. She noticed the window blinds swaying. Now she felt as though some presence in the house was spying on her. She and George looked for help. They found someone who offered to chase "bad spirits" out of the house for $140 a hour—but success was not guaranteed. They kept looking. That's when Nickell heard about the case. He agreed to visit George and Mary.

Nickell listened to George and Mary describe the frightening happenings. He didn't accuse them of making up their stories, or of imagining what had happened. He took their story seriously. But he also told them that "the least likely explanation for something like this is a ghost" because there is no solid, scientific evidence of ghosts. If the happenings in the house could be explained in natural, ordinary ways, those explanations would be more likely than a haunting.

Next, Nickell looked for possible natural explanations for the things that had happened. When he learned that only one door had mysteriously slammed shut, and only in the summer, he pointed out an air conditioner mounted on a nearby wall. There was also a fireplace with an open chimney flue in the room. The working of the air conditioner, or a gust of wind traveling down the flue, could change the air pressure in the room, and that could make a door move on its own.

The bright shape that had moved across the kitchen could have been a car's headlights shining through a window in another room. George and Mary were new to the house at the time. They didn't have much experience with the special sights and sounds that every house has. And the gruesome stories they had heard about the house might have prepared their minds for thoughts of haunting.

Not long after Nickell's visit, Mary made a discovery of her own. She found that throwing back the covers on her bed made the window blinds sway. No longer was she afraid of an unknown presence haunting her new home.

What about the child's giggling that Mary heard? It happened at night. When people are tired, their senses can play tricks on them. Mary might have been thinking about the little boy who was supposed to have died in the house. If she heard an unexpected noise, it might have sounded like a child's voice. Finally, George and Mary had five pets, and one of them might have made a sound.

Beyond the Haunted House

Houses aren't the only things that can be haunted. Spooky happenings have been reported in all kinds of buildings. Ghost lore has tales of haunted ships, trains, automobiles, and carriages. Even certain subway stations in the Asian nation of Singapore are rumored to be haunted by headless ghosts. Just about anything that a person can die in, it seems, can become the setting for a ghost.

The Sequin Island lighthouse in Georgetown, Maine, has a grim legend. The story goes that a lighthouse keeper brought his bride to the lonely spot. To cheer her up, he had a piano brought to the island. But the woman had only one piece of music. She played it over and over and over until her husband went crazy and took an ax to both the piano and the piano player. That unlucky tune still echoes through the lighthouse from time to time.

For many years the Mississippi River was a highway for riverboats carrying cargo and passengers. In 1890, Charles and Mary Greene founded a riverboat company that still operates several passenger boats. One of them, the *Delta Queen,* was Mary Greene's home for a long time before her death in 1949. She was not just an owner—she was the boat's pilot. Some of those who have worked and traveled on the *Delta Queen* claim that Mary is still aboard.

One first mate on the boat recalled being woken at night by a whisper in his ear. No one was in the room. Then he heard the sound of a slamming door. He followed it to the engine room and discovered a leak. Water was pouring into the boat. He thinks

Does the kind ghost of the *Delta Queen*'s former pilot still keep a protective eye on the vessel she once loved?

that Mary's ghost keeps an eye on the vessel she loved, and that Mary woke him when there was trouble. On another occasion, a television crew was making a documentary about the *Delta Queen*. A cameraman was filming some old photos of Mary and other people in the boat's history. He became very upset and told the rest of the crew that when he looked through his camera at Mary's picture, she was not just an old photo—she was alive!

The *Delta Queen* is a haunted ship. A ghost ship is different—the entire ship is a phantom. Ghost ships are usually said to be apparitions of real vessels that sank, usually in a violent manner. The story of the *Lady Lovibond* is a classic example.

On Friday, February 13, 1748, the *Lady Lovibond* was at sea off the English coast. The captain had just gotten married, and his bride was aboard the ship. One of the crewmen was in love with the bride, and in a fit of anger or despair he ran the three-masted schooner into a treacherous area of shallow water called the Goodwin Sands. The ship was wrecked. Everyone aboard her died. Fifty years later, the phantom of the *Lady Lovibond* was spotted by two other ships. The ghost ship was seen again after another fifty years had passed. This time, it looked so real that people on shore sent out lifeboats to rescue survivors. The *Lady Lovibond's* ghost last sailed in 1948. That year, only one person claimed to have seen her.

Amityville Horror or Amityville Hoax?

One of the most famous hauntings in modern America happened in the town of Amityville, New York. Like many hauntings, it came after tragic, violent death.

On November 13, 1974, six members of the DeFeo family were shot to death as they slept in their Amityville home. The only family member left alive was a son named Ronald Jr. He confessed to the killings and went to prison. The next year, George and Kathy Lutz moved into the DeFeo house with their three children.

The Lutzes soon discovered that life in "the murder house" was terrifying. Some evil power lurked there. It was strong enough to tear a door from its hinges and bend the locks of windows. Green slime dripped from a ceiling. In the middle of winter, a room filled with houseflies. Something with red eyes peered through the windows. When the Lutzes went outside to investigate, they found prints in the snow. They were the prints of cloven, or split, animal hoofs—and some people think that the devil has cloven hoofs! The police were called but could do nothing.

Just twenty-eight days after moving into the house, the Lutzes moved out. Their story appeared on local television news and caused a sensation. A publishing company hired a writer named Jay Anson to produce a book about it. *The Amityville Horror: A True Story* was published in 1977. It was a best seller that was made into a movie in 1979. The movie led to a string of sequels for theaters, video, and television. Many people grew up believing that *The Amityville Horror was* "a true story."

But there were problems with the story right from the start. In 1978, investigators found that the police had never been called to the house. And on the night when the Lutzes claimed to have found the cloven hoofprints, there was no snow in Amityville. Other people noticed that in places the Lutzes' story sounded a lot like scenes from the frightening 1973 movie *The Exorcist.*

People who lived in the Amityville house after the Lutzes left reported no unusual experiences. James and Barbara Cromarty, who bought the house, showed investigators the doors and windows that the Lutzes said had been severely damaged by the evil

After six people were murdered in this house in Amityville, New York, the new owners claimed to be besieged by green slime, hordes of flies, and other evil omens. A book about their ordeal, *The Amityville Horror,* became a best seller and inspired a movie.

ghost or spirit. The hardware, paint, and varnish on the doors and windows were old and had not been disturbed.

The truth came from an unexpected source—William Webber, the attorney for Ronald DeFeo Jr., the confessed killer. Webber came forward and admitted that he and the Lutzes had invented the whole story of the Amityville haunting. They hoped to make money from a book and movie deal. "We were creating something the public wanted to hear about," Webber said.

George and Kathy Lutz during a book tour for *The Amityville Horror* in 1979, before their story was revealed as a money-making hoax.

Two lawsuits brought the hoax into the open. Webber sued the Lutzes, saying that they had broken their agreement to share the profits. The Cromartys also sued the Lutzes, writer Anson, and the publishing company. The Cromartys said that the fake haunting story had destroyed their right to privacy in their home because so many people came onto the property to see the "haunted" house.

Amityville turned into a big embarrassment for some ghost believers. They worried that the public would think all haunted houses are hoaxes, or that people who experience hauntings would not report them for fear of being called fakers. But a few diehard believers still refuse to accept that *The Amityville Horror* is fiction, not "a true story." Tragic murders really did take place in the house, they say. Even if the Lutzes were lying, who can prove that the house isn't haunted anyway?

No one can prove that the Amityville house isn't haunted. But there's no good reason to think that it is.

Séances, meetings to summon spirits, became enormously
popular in the nineteenth century. Such meetings were
sometimes called table·tipping sessions because the spirits were
said to make the table rock, tip, or rattle against the floor.

Spirit Rappers and Toe Crackers

Belief in ghosts faded during the eighteenth century—at least among educated people in Europe and the United States. Many of them thought that all accounts of ghosts and hauntings were works of imagination, and that only common, uneducated folk took spirits seriously. Daniel Defoe, the English author of *Robinson Crusoe,* felt that way. He called ghost reports "good old Tales which serve to make up Winter-Evening Conversation" and "the bewildered Imaginations and Dreams of Ignorant People."

Ghosts seemed to be losing their hold on the living. But in the nineteenth century, the spirits would return, stronger than ever. These spirits were not the gruesome, chain-rattling ghosts of old stories. They were messengers bringing news of life after death.

The Amazing Fox Sisters

It all started with two young girls, Katherine and Margaretta Fox, called Kate and Maggie. They were about eleven and thirteen years old in 1848. The Fox family lived in a two-room house in Hydesville, New York.

Kate (left) and Maggie Fox were teenagers when they launched the spiritualist movement in the United States. The sisters claimed they received messages from the spirit world in the form of knocking sounds.

Strange rapping or knocking sounds woke the Foxes one night in March. The sounds soon stopped, but they came back on the nights that followed. The sounds seemed to follow the girls around—they never happened when the girls were gone. What could be causing them? The girls' mother, Margaret Fox, solved the mystery. The raps were communications from an invisible spirit!

What made Margaret Fox think that the unusual sounds were spirit communications? Maybe the time and place in which she lived led her to think that way.

Hydesville was in a part of New York State that had seen many religious movements. Seventh Day Adventism and Mormonism are just two of the religions that came out of the area in the nineteenth century. Local people were filled with enthusiasm for new beliefs, including spiritualism, or communicating with the dead.

A century before, a Swedish religious writer named Emanuel Swedenborg had described the afterlife, the place of the soul after death. He claimed that instead of a single heaven and a single hell, as taught by traditional Christian faiths, the spirits of the dead pass through many stages of the afterlife. In some stages, they can communicate with the living. Swedenborg said that he had gotten his information from the spirits during trances.

Trances were one form of hypnotism, which was called mesmerism in the nineteenth century. Part science, part entertainment, hypnotism was extremely popular. Crowds filled halls for demonstrations of it. Often the hypnotists put their subjects into trances, which are deep states of partial awareness. After coming out of the trances, some subjects reported encounters with spiritual beings.

In 1847, just a year before the rappings at the Fox home, a hypnotist named Andrew Jackson Davis published a book about the spirits called *The Principles of Nature, Her Divine Revelations, and a Voice to Mankind.* Davis was from Poughkeepsie, not far from Hydesville. Margaret Fox, who was interested in spiritualism, could easily have read his book, or heard of it.

When Margaret Fox realized that the spirits were speaking (or knock-

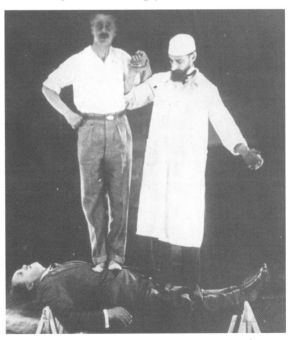

In a 1930 demonstration, two men stand on the body of a third, who has been hypnotized. Hypnosis was a fascinating, crowd-pleasing phenomenon.

ing) through her daughters, she called neighbors to share the experience. The spirits rapped out the ages of everyone in the room—one rap for each year. Soon the Foxes came up with a system of spirit communication. To get the answer to a question, someone would recite the letters of the alphabet. At the correct letter, the spirits would rap. This way they could spell out words and sentences, although it took a long time. (Sometimes the questioner helped by guessing what the spirits were trying to spell and jumping ahead to the right letter.)

The spirit rappings caused an uproar. Other people had claimed to see and hear spirits when they were in trances, but the raps at the Fox home were something new—loud sounds that *everyone* could hear. Soon the Fox home was crowded with visitors from morning until midnight. Leah Fish, a married sister of Maggie and Kate, moved home and started managing the crowds. Then Leah decided that Maggie and Kate should give a public demonstration.

Four hundred people packed the demonstration hall in Rochester, New York. Not all of them were believers. Some were certain that the "spirits" were a trick and that the girls were somehow making the noises. One man even stood before the audience and loudly cracked the joints in his toes. That, he declared, was the secret of the raps. But most people found Kate and Maggie's demonstrations convincing. Soon the Fox sisters were living in New York City and charging fees for private spirit readings and public performances. They quickly became celebrities. But they weren't the only ones talking to the spirits.

Spirits Everywhere

Wherever Kate and Maggie gave a demonstration, people in the audience soon discovered that they, too, could be mediums,

with the power to communicate with spirits. In New York, Pennsylvania, and all over the land, friends and neighbors formed "spirit circles" in their parlors. If they couldn't summon up a rapping spirit, perhaps they would get a table-tipping spirit that made the furniture rock and bump. Or they might discover that group members could go into trances and talk with the spirits that way.

At a 1937 séance, a dead Native American named Moon Trail speaks through English medium Horace S. Hambling. For some reason, many mediums claimed to have Indians as their "spirit guides."

Before long, there were millions of spiritualists in the United States alone. They held lectures and demonstrations, summer camps, and state and national meetings. Whole communities were founded upon them. One of the first was the town of Lily Dale, close to the birthplace of American spiritualism in New York State. It got its start in 1879 and is still the home of a spiritualist community.

Spiritualism was popular in Great Britain, too. Table-turning sessions, where people sat around a table and the spirits made the table rotate, were common. *The Spiritualist,* an English weekly magazine of the 1870s, told people how to hold séances.

Ectoplasm leaves a medium's mouth during a séance. Mediums faked ectoplasm with various substances, including cheesecloth and sheeps' stomachs.

As more mediums practiced their trade, spirit activity grew more dramatic. Spirits rattled tambourines, played trumpets, and banged drums. Mediums spoke in strange voices—the voices of the spirits themselves. Pale, glowing forms appeared. Often these took the form of white spirit hands. Sometimes these hands would touch the sitters.

Spiritualists said that the eerie forms were made of ectoplasm, a mysterious cloudy gas that emerged from mediums during trances. Ectoplasm was spirit energy that took on a physical form so that it could be seen. At the end of the séance, it disappeared because the energy went back into the medium.

There had always been people who said that they could see or hear spirits. But the rappings, thumps, spirit voices, and ectoplasm of the new spiritualists were public signs, and physical ones. People felt that a window had opened onto the mysteries of life and death. The spirits who had "passed over" into the afterlife had wisdom to share with the living. Their communications were proof that the human spirit lives on after death. All of this was tremendously exciting.

Anyone might be thrilled by a chance to talk to loved ones who had died, or share the secrets of the dead. But people in the late nineteenth and early twentieth centuries were drawn to spiritualism for special reasons.

First, spiritualism was open to women. It was a way for them to take part in public life, even to earn money, at a time when women had few activities beyond housework and child rearing. Séances and spiritualist meetings gave many women their only chances to make speeches and meet new people.

Second, spiritualism helped heal the misery of people who lost sons, husbands, and brothers in several large wars. The Civil War tore apart the United States in the 1860s. World War I raged in Europe from 1914 to 1918. Tremendous numbers of lives were lost. After these conflicts, many mourners turned to spiritualism as a way of dealing with their sorrow.

Spiritualism meant different things to different people. For some, especially those who had lost faith in traditional religions, it became a new religion called the Spiritualist Church. Today, people still follow this faith. In the United States, most of them are part of the National Association of Spiritualist Churches. In Great Britain they belong to several groups, such as the Spiritualist National Union. There are Spiritualist churches in many other countries, including Japan, Australia, Italy, Germany, and South Africa.

But some people saw no need to join the Spiritualist Church. They found that spiritualism fit in with the religious beliefs they already held. Still other people came to spiritualism from a scientific point of view. In 1882, people interested in the serious study of the supernatural founded the Society for Psychical Research (SPR) in Great Britain. The SPR is still active. So is the American Society for Psychical Research (ASPR), which started in 1885. In the 1920s Harry Price, the investigator of Borley Rectory, set up his own National Laboratory of Psychical Research.

Sir Arthur Conan Doyle—physician, author, and creator of the famous fictional detective Sherlock Holmes—firmly believed in the existence of ghosts and spirit communication.

A number of well-known people became spiritualists. In England, famous believers included Queen Victoria and Sir Arthur Conan Doyle, the creator of the fictional detective Sherlock Holmes. But other people were skeptical. Some of the skeptics became debunkers. They set out to expose spirit mediums as frauds—and sometimes they succeeded.

Fakes and Frauds

Right from the start, people questioned the truth of spiritualism. Elisha Kent Kane, a famous explorer from a well-known Philadelphia family, fell in love with one of the first American spiritualists, Maggie Fox. But he doubted that her spirit rappings were genuine. In one letter to her, he wrote, "I believe the only thing I ever was afraid of was, this confounded thing [the truth about the rapping] being found out."

Many mediums were frauds. They browsed through catalogs for equipment to trick their customers. Two popular items were glow-in-the-dark paint for preparing apparitions and thin black rods for writing on ceilings or moving objects without being seen (nearly all séances took place in dark rooms, or at least dim ones). Mediums could also buy special shoes that produced rapping sounds without visible movement of the feet.

Experienced mediums told newcomers that when visiting a town for the first time, they should go to the cemetery and learn the names and dates of people who had recently died. Relatives of the newly dead were likely to be among the medium's customers. In time, a document called the Blue Book was passed around among mediums. It listed important facts about the people in each community. When a medium gave a séance in a community, folks would be astonished by the medium's knowledge of local affairs—knowledge supposedly gained from the spirits.

Sometimes mediums suffered public embarrassment. The Davenport brothers from Buffalo, New York, began performing as mediums in 1854. Ten years later they traveled to England. Their most famous demonstration involved a large box and a number of musical instruments. The two brothers would be tied up so that they couldn't move, then shut into a box with the instruments. They would summon the spirits to play the instruments. Then the box would be opened, showing that the brothers were still tightly bound.

Professional magicians knew that many knots could be secretly untied, with skill and practice. Escaping from ropes and knots is one of a master illusionist's most valuable tricks. Magicians set out to debunk the Davenport brothers. They started performing the same marvels as the Davenports, then showing that they were done by rope tricks, not spirits. For the Davenports, the end came when two amateur magicians started following them from show to show. The magicians insisted on tying the brothers with a knot that could not be undone. This debunking ruined the demonstration. Angry audiences demanded their money back.

A few years later, the Fox sisters made a shocking confession. In 1888, Maggie Fox told an audience at the New York Academy of Music that she and Kate had lied for forty years about the spirit rappings. Maggie took off her shoes and showed how she made the raps by cracking the joint of her big toe, which had become large with use. The sound was loud enough to be heard throughout the theater.

Maggie said that Kate could do it, too. They had started it as a joke. Then they had learned how to fool people into thinking that the raps came from someplace other than their feet. When they cracked their toes, they simply looked at a point on the wall or the floor, or at a piece of furniture. This technique (professional magicians call it misdirection) made people think the sound was coming from that point.

Kate was in the theater that night. She agreed that everything Maggie said was true. The raps had been phony from start to finish!

Was this confession the end of spiritualism? Not at all. Believers accused Maggie and Kate of lying about faking the raps. By now, the two sisters were poor, sad, and sick. Some people said they had made up their confession for money. Others said they did it to strike out at their sister Leah, who was rich and successful. A year later, desperate to earn money again as a medium, Maggie wrote that she had made up the confession, and that the raps were genuine spirit noises all along. But by this time, no one cared about her or Kate.

A professional magician (left) demonstrates a medium's trick. The man on the right thinks he holds the magician's feet and hands, but the magician manages to ring a "spirit bell."

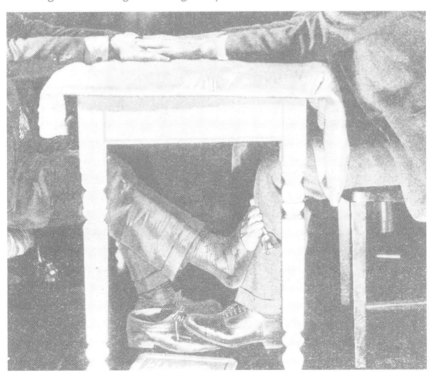

At a 1926 U.S. Senate hearing aimed at exposing fake spiritualists, Houdini shows tablets on which ghosts supposedly wrote messages in chalk.

Other mediums confessed to fraud, or were caught in the act. Professional magicians played a big role in exposing fake mediums because they hated seeing the skills and methods of the trained illusionist used to support false claims of spirit communication. Harry Houdini, the most famous magician of his day, loved debunking mediums' tricks. He talked to elderly mediums who told him how they had fooled their customers over the years. Some of them had faked ectoplasm with sheep intestines or pieces of cloth.

Yet no matter how many mediums were shown to be fake, spiritualists continued to believe in communication with the dead. They felt that even if one medium was a hoax, that didn't mean the next one wasn't genuine. And not all mediums were shown to be frauds.

Daniel D. Home was one of the most famous mediums of the 1860s and 1870s. He performed for the emperor of France, the czar of Russia, and several British scientists. In his most remarkable demonstrations, Home appeared to rise into the air, carried by invisible spirits. Skeptics and professional magicians have read firsthand accounts of these séances. They have suggested ways that Home could have faked his performances, but they do not *know* that he did. One thing we do know is that Home was never caught in a hoax. Was he a genuine medium? Only his spirit knows—and it's not telling.

Annette Martin is one of many modern psychics, mediums, and channelers who claim to be able to communicate with the spirits of the dead.

Modern Mediums and Ghost Hunters

R appings and ectoplasm have been out of fashion for years, but spirit communication is as popular as ever. Today, many people claim that they can contact the dead. Some offer their services to the public as psychics, channelers, or spirit mediums. Most of the time, their powers are mental, not physical. Instead of producing sounds or moving tables, they communicate with the spirits through inner voices or visions that no one else can hear or see.

Direct Line to the Dead?

Paranormal investigator Joe Nickell thinks that the modern style of spirit communication is safer for mediums than the old-fashioned floating ectoplasm, because it makes fakes harder to expose. Nickell has studied some modern psychics and mediums who have appeared on television. He found that the readings they give are a lot like the acts of mentalists, professional magicians who do mind-reading tricks but don't claim to have supernatural powers or spirit guides.

One method mentalists use is to speak in the form of questions, not statements. A mentalist might say, "Are you thinking about a woman you miss?" instead of "You are thinking about a woman you miss." Often, when the subject answers the question, he or she unknowingly reveals information that the mentalist can use. Another method is to give insights in very broad terms that could mean a lot of different things. A statement like "You are wondering if you made the right choice" could apply to almost anyone.

Mentalists also repeat their "hits," the things they've gotten right. The mentalist uses slightly different words each time, so that the repeated statements seem like different insights, even if they are not very different. The subject will remember a lot of agreeing with the mentalist. But the mentalist will quickly drop any mistakes or "misses" from the conversation, so that they will be forgotten.

The flicker of an eyelid or shift of a gaze tells a lot to a skilled mentalist, who often can perform a convincing mind-reading act.

Good mentalists are highly skilled at reading our facial expressions, our body language, and our tones of voice. To a mentalist, a tiny flicker of the subject's eyelids or a drawn breath can suggest that the mentalist has hit on something the subject thinks is important. Using these clues, mentalists produce results that seem like magic—or like the readings of a psychic or medium.

A psychologist and skeptic named Michael Shermer wondered how closely a mentalist's skills might match those of a psychic. He put himself to the test in an experiment he called "Psychic for a Day." Shermer gave himself twenty-four hours to learn the basics of cold readings—a mentalist's term for giving readings to complete strangers.

One cold-reading technique is memorizing lists of the most common names for men and women in different age groups. This improves a mentalist's chances of correctly "reading" the name or initial of a subject's friend or family member. Shermer also practiced the mentalist's trick of talking about things that most people are likely to have in their homes: photo albums, old letters, a piece of jewelry with emotional meaning. If a mentalist mentions such an object, the subject usually says, "Yes, I have that!" Finally, mentalists know that people who come to a reading are usually interested in love, money, health, career, or family. And if the reading involves contact with spirits, subjects expect to hear from the spirits of people close to them, such as parents or loved ones, not from more distant figures.

For a television science show, Shermer posed as a card reader, astrologer, palm reader, psychic, and spirit medium. All five of the women he "read" said that his readings were good. Shermer did the experiment to show that it is not hard to make people think you have special knowledge about their lives and problems, if you use the methods of cold reading.

Do studies like Nickell's and Shermer's mean that psychics and mediums are fakes? No. They just mean that with a little practice, ordinary people can get results like psychics, but without claiming to be in contact with the dead.

What happens when a reading goes wrong? When the Fox sisters made mistakes or had trouble answering a question, they said that someone in the room didn't believe in the spirits, or was against them. That's why their spirit rappers couldn't perform properly. Modern mediums still do the same thing, often saying that the "negative energy" of a skeptic blocks the use of psychic powers. Maybe this is true—but it's very handy for psychics. If someone questions the correctness of a reading, it must be the questioner's fault, not the psychic's!

Still, some "communications" from the spirit world *are* hard to explain. Mary Roach is a writer who investigated spirit communication for her book *Spook: Science Tackles the Afterlife*. "I am skeptical by nature," Roach says. At the University of Arizona, she met with a spirit medium named Allison DuBois, who says that she started "seeing dead people" as a child, when she had a vision of her grandfather after his death. DuBois made several statements about Roach's dead mother. None of them was very accurate. Then, after the reading was over, DuBois suddenly said, "I'm showing a metal hourglass, that you turn over. Does your brother have one?"

Roach was amazed. Her brother collects hourglasses. She found it hard to think that the comment was just luck, or accident. Yet she also remembered that the comments about her mother didn't fit, and she wondered why her mother's spirit would show DuBois an hourglass. "Maybe that *was* my mother coming through," she wrote. "But what's the meaning of it? Why would one of my brother's hourglasses be the image she chose to present to me?"

For many people, the question of talking to the dead remains open. Some think that spirit communication may be a kind of brain activity that science doesn't yet understand. Psychics and scientists, sometimes working together, are exploring this paranormal frontier. They are part of a new wave of ghost research.

Twenty-First-Century Ghost Hunters

Paranormal research is booming. From thrill seekers to mainstream scientists, it has something for everyone. Operators offer "ghost tours" of spots said to be haunted. Some tours include overnight stays in cemeteries, battlefields, or old movie theaters where ghosts lurk.

Ghost hunting is big business. Hundreds, maybe thousands, of people and companies offer their services as ghost finders, or even

Today's ghost hunters use high-tech tools such as meters that detect metal and electricity, which some investigators believe are indicators of paranormal activity. This investigation is taking place on the grounds of a monastery in Rhode Island.

ghost removers. Some of these paranormalists follow in the footsteps of Harry Price. He was one of the first to measure and record physical phenomena, such as sudden temperature drops, that took place at séances or in haunted houses. He developed a "ghost hunter's kit" that included a thermometer, a camera, a tape measure to check rooms for hidden compartments, and fingerprint powder (not just to look for fingerprints, but to dust around objects so that he could see if they were moved).

Today, a ghost hunter's kit might contain night-vision goggles, a digital camera equipped for night photography, motion detectors (like those used in security systems), an electromagnetic-field detector (electricians use these to check for bad wiring, but some paranormal researchers think ghosts cause changes in electromagnetic fields), and walkie-talkies for communication among team members. And thanks to the Internet, ghost believers and hunters can now share information with thousands of others around the world. News of a ghost sighting brings people flocking to the spot.

Some ghost hunting happens in the laboratory. In recent years, experts in engineering, brain science, and psychology have offered new answers to the age-old question: Why do people see ghosts?

An English engineer named Vic Tandy thinks ghosts might be sound waves. To be more exact, he thinks that certain kinds of sound waves affect the human body. Someone who experiences these effects but doesn't know the cause might think something supernatural is happening.

Tandy started studying sound waves after a strange experience in his own lab years ago. He felt uneasy and saw a gray presence out of the corner of his eye, but nothing was there. Others had the same experience. Tandy had a fencing foil (a fine, pointed sword) in his lab and noticed that it was vibrating strangely. He thought that the vibration might be caused by infrasound—a very low-frequency sound wave that human ears can't hear. He discovered that a new fan in the building was shaking, creating an infrasound wave. When it was fixed, the eerie sensations vanished.

Since then, Tandy and other researchers have experimented with infrasound. It makes many people uncomfortable, or cold, or sick, although they don't know why. It can also make human eyeballs vibrate slightly, which causes hallucinations.

Infrasound is produced by all kinds of things—church organs, machinery, animals such as tigers and elephants, wheels rolling on a distant road, and even such common and simple events as air moving across walls. In the right conditions, infrasound waves form "pools," spots where they are especially intense. Tandy believes these waves could be the cause of at least some "hauntings."

A researcher in Canada thinks that electromagnetic fields (EMFs) might be part of the explanation. Michael Persinger is a neuroscientist, an expert in how the brain works. He has studied EMFs, which are both natural (produced by the earth's magnetism and by energy from the sun) and man-made (caused by electrical equipment and wiring). EMFs change often. They can be high in one place or time, low in another.

Persinger has found that some places where people report seeing ghosts or feeling haunted have high EMFs. In his lab, he is studying the effects of EMFs on the brain. He is one of several researchers who have found that electromagnetism applied to the brain can make people have hallucinations. Often these hallucinations feel like being haunted, or being suddenly afraid, or having a paranormal or mystical experience.

Using a special helmet, Persinger has given mild EMF bursts to volunteers. Eighty percent of them sense a "presence" nearby. But even if Persinger can create ghosts in the lab, do EMFs explain all ghost sightings?

A headless drummer boy and a spectral bagpiper are said to haunt Scotland's Edinburgh Castle, the scene of recent paranormal research.

A British psychologist named Richard Wiseman has used hundreds of volunteers to study two of the most haunted spots in the British Isles: Edinburgh Castle in Scotland and Hampton Court Palace in England. They measured temperatures and EMFs. They also recorded any unusual or paranormal experiences—such as a feeling of being watched or touched, a sudden chill, and the sight of shadowy forms. One young volunteer who spent a night alone in a vault in Edinburgh Castle reported hearing breathing, as though someone were in the room with her.

When Wiseman looked at the results, he found that the volunteers reported more strange experiences in the parts of the buildings that have been rumored to be haunted—sometimes for hundreds of years. This suggests, he says, that hauntings are real.

But maybe ghosts are not. "Hauntings exist, in the sense that places exist where people reliably have unusual experiences," Wiseman said. "The existence of ghosts is a way of explaining these experiences." He thinks that at least some of the volunteers' experiences could have been caused by physical factors such as darkness, chill, and EMF variations in the "most haunted" spots.

Did we create the idea of ghosts to explain strange feelings and experiences that have natural, physical causes—causes that we simply do not sense or recognize? Some ghost believers think that natural forces such as EMFs and infrasound *are* connected with hauntings. Maybe, they say, ghosts and spirits produce these forms of energy. After all, a scientific explanation for some ghost reports doesn't mean that science has explained away *all* ghosts.

Bridge between the living and the dead, or figment
of the imagination? Ghosts and spirits have terrified and
tantalized people for thousands of years, even though
their existence has yet to be proved.

What Do You Think?

Who, or what, was the Bell Witch? In the opening pages of this book, you read about that famous haunting on the Tennessee frontier. Later, you learned that the Bell Witch was said to be the ghost of an old woman named Kate, who thought John Bell had cheated her out of some property. Did you wonder where this information came from?

The first public record of the Bell Witch was a brief mention in a book published in 1886, two generations after the haunting ended in 1821. *The Goodspeed History of Tennessee* said, "A remarkable occurrence, which attracted widespread interest, was connected with the family of John Bell, who settled in what is now known as Adams Station about 1804. So great was the excitement that people came from hundreds of miles around to witness the manifestations of what was popularly known as the 'Bell Witch.'"

But if hundreds of people flocked to the Bell farm to see the haunting, they left no mention of it in a newspaper, diary, or letter written at the time of the haunting. General Andrew Jackson was said to have come to the farm. He was a public figure whose comings and goings were noticed, but there is no evidence that he

A vengeful witch named Kate was blamed for the Bell haunting—yet Kate was still alive, not a ghost, at the time of the supposed haunting.

ever visited the Bell farm or said a word about it.

What about old Kate? The neighbor woman who bought property from Bell lived longer than he did, so her ghost could not have haunted his farm. It seems that Kate somehow got mixed up in the story years after the original haunting.

No one knows where the author of the *Goodspeed History* got his information about the Bell Witch, but it could have been local folklore or old stories. The book contains a lot of those. The next report of the Bell Witch haunting came in 1894, when a printer named Martin Ingram published *The Authenticated History of the Bell Witch.*

Ingram got his information from a member of the Bell family, who gave him an old diary titled "My Family's Troubles." That diary was supposedly written by Richard Bell, Betsy Bell's little brother, who was six years old when the haunting began. But Richard didn't write the diary *during* the haunting. He wrote it twenty-five years after the mysterious events ended.

That diary is the only report of the Bell Witch haunting that was written by someone who claimed to witness the haunting. Do you think it is a reliable source of information about an extraordinary claim? Can you think of other possible explanations for strange behavior and events at the Bell farm? Some of the phenomena, such as noises and flying bedclothes, sound like poltergeist activity.

Could teenage Betsy Bell have been responsible for the disturbances?

It's possible that Richard Bell was confused about what he remembered. Martin Ingram could have exaggerated the story of the Bell Witch to make a more exciting book. But something unusual seems to have happened at the Bell farm. Perhaps researchers will one day discover that the place where the farm once stood is haunted by infrasound waves, or electromagnetic fields, or the ghost of a long-dead witch.

Maybe the question to ask about ghosts is not: Are they real? Maybe the right question is: Why do we care about ghosts and spirits?

Even someone who doesn't believe in ghosts might shiver with dread at the thought of a spectral hand reaching out from beyond the grave to torment the living.

Ghosts have a powerful hold on our thoughts and imaginations because they seem to offer a clue about the great mysteries of life and death. And while the sight of a ghost may be frightening and disturbing, it is also thrilling. Ghosts might be seen as signs that life—or some kind of existence—goes on after death.

For thousands of years, people have told of encounters with spirits of the dead. Today, almost a third of all American adults believe in ghosts, according to a 2005 Gallup poll. But since there is no final proof either way about ghosts and spirits, you will have to decide for yourself.

Who knows? Someday you may see a ghost yourself, if you are lucky. Or unlucky . . .

Glossary

apparition Mysterious appearance; ghost.

debunker One who proves that a supernatural or paranormal claim is false, or at least suspicious, by providing a natural explanation, pointing out holes or weaknesses in the claim, or exposing a hoax.

medium One who claims to be able to communicate with the dead.

percipient A person who sees a ghost or has a supernatural experience.

poltergeist "Noisy ghost" that makes noises or moves objects. Episodes of poltergeist activity are usually temporary and often connected with young people, especially girls.

psychic One who claims to have extraordinary mental powers, such as reading minds, predicting the future, or communicating with spirits.

séance A session in which people attempt to communicate with a ghost, using a medium or a device that the ghost can move to spell out words.

skeptic One who requires extraordinary proof of extraordinary claims and uses critical thinking to test statements.

spiritualism The belief that it is possible to communicate with the dead, or the practice of communicating with the dead.

For Further Research

Books

Banks, Cameron. *Haunted History: America's Most Haunted*. New York: Scholastic, 2002.

*Barker, Dan. *Maybe Yes, Maybe No: A Guide for Young Skeptics*. Amherst, NY: Prometheus Books, 1993.

Canadeo, Anne. *Fact or Fiction Files: Ghosts*. New York: Walker, 1990.

Cohen, Daniel, and Susan Cohen. *Hauntings and Horrors: The Ultimate Guide to Spooky America*. New York: Dutton, 2002.

Deem, James, and True Kelley. *How to Find a Ghost*. New York: Avon, 1990.

De La Rosa, Sheila. *Ghost Files: Creepy . . . but True?* New York: Disney Press, 1997.

Editors of USA Weekend. *I Never Believed in Ghosts Until . . . : 100 Real-Life Encounters*. New York: McGraw-Hill, 1992.

Emert, Phyllis Raybin. *Ghosts, Hauntings, and Mysterious Happenings*. New York: Tom Doherty Associates, 1994.

*Gardner, Robert. *What's So Super about the Supernatural?* Brookfield, CT: Twenty-First Century Press, 1998.

Guy, John. *Ghosts*. Milwaukee: Gareth Stevens, 2006.

Krohn, Katherine E. *Haunted Houses*. Mankato, MN: Edge Books, 2006.

Martin, Michael. *Ghosts*. Mankato, MN: Capstone Press, 2005.

Netzley, Patricia. *Fact or Fiction? Haunted Houses*. San Diego: Greenhaven Press, 2000.

Ogden, Tom. *The Complete Idiot's Guide to Ghosts and Hauntings*. 2nd ed. Indianapolis: Alpha Books, 2004.

O'Neill, Terry, ed. *Fact or Fiction? Ghosts and Poltergeists*. San Diego: Greenhaven Press, 2002.

*Ruchlis, Hy. *How Do You Know It's True?* Amherst, NY: Prometheus Books, 1991.

---

*Book or Web site that will help develop critical thinking

www.csicop.org

> *CSICOP (the Committee for the Scientific Investigation of Claims of the Paranormal) is a good place to see critical thinking applied to supernatural claims. Its searchable online archive contains articles about ghosts, hauntings, and spiritualism. Many articles tell how CSICOP members investigated those claims.

www.paranormal.about.com/od/ghostsandhauntings/

> This "Ghosts and Hauntings" page is part of about.com's Paranormal Phenomena section. It has links to archives of ghost photos and videos, descriptions of ghost walks and tours, tips for ghost hunters, a catalog of haunted places, and "True Ghost Stories," an extensive file of ghost reports.

www.ghostmag.com

> The Web site of *Ghost!* (a magazine "for the ghost-hunting enthusiast") has reports from the "ghostologists" who investigate battlefields, haunted hotels, and other spooky sites.

www.invink.com

> Invisible Ink is an online bookstore for books about ghosts and hauntings, both nonfiction and fiction. A special section lists and describes books for young readers.

www.snu.org.uk

> The Spiritualists' National Union in Great Britain calls itself "probably the largest spiritualist organization in the world." Its Web site describes the history and ideas of the modern religion based on spiritualism.

www.skeptiseum.org/exhibits/ghostsspirits

> *The online Skeptical Museum of the Paranormal is run by CSICOP. The Ghosts and Spirits section focuses mainly on spiritualism. It has brief, illustrated accounts of spiritualist history and lore.

www.discoverychannel.co.uk/paranormal/index.shtml

> The Discovery Channel Web site has a "Psychic and Paranormal" page. There you'll find sections on the spirit world, the world's most haunted places, and ghost hunting, as well as "Jargon Buster," a dictionary of supernatural and paranormal terms.

www.haunted-places.com/International.htm

This list of international haunted places covers all continents. It has brief summaries of dozens of reported hauntings around the world and links to other sites.

www.skepdic.com/ghosts

The Skeptic's Dictionary is an Internet reference that covers supernatural and paranormal topics "from abracadabra to zombies." Its "Ghost" page has links to online news articles about apparitions and ghost research. *The Skeptic's Dictionary* also offers a set of mini lessons in critical thinking.

Selected Bibliography

The author found these resources especially helpful when researching and writing this book:

Brandon, Ruth. *The Spiritualists: The Passion for the Occult in the Nineteenth and Twentieth Centuries*. New York: Knopf, 1983.

Brown, Nicola, Carolyn Burdett, and Pamela Thurschwell, eds. *The Victorian Supernatural*. New York: Cambridge University Press, 2004.

Cavendish, Richard, ed. *Man, Myth, & Magic: The Illustrated Encyclopedia of Mythology, Religion, and the Unknown*. 21 vols. New York: Marshall Cavendish, 1995.

Danelek, J. Allen. *The Case for Ghosts*. Woodbury, MN: Llewellyn, 2006.

Finucane, Ronald. *Ghosts: Appearances of the Dead and Cultural Transformation*. Amherst, NY: Prometheus Books, 1996.

Houdini, Harry. *A Magician among the Spirits*. New York: Arno Press, 1972.

Houran, James, and Rense Lange, eds. *Hauntings and Poltergeists: Multidisciplinary Perspectives*. Jefferson, NC: McFarland & Co., 2001.

Randi, James. *An Encyclopedia of Frauds, Claims, and Hoaxes of the Occult and Supernatural*. New York: St. Martin's Press, 1995.

Roach, Mary. *Spook: Science Tackles the Afterlife*. New York: Norton, 2005.

Weisberg, Barbara. *Talking to the Dead: Kate and Maggie Fox and the Rise of Spiritualism*. San Francisco: Harper, 2004.

Zimmer, Carl. *Soul Made Flesh: The Discovery of the Brain and How It Changed the World*. New York: Free Press, 2004.

Notes

Chapter 1: Ghosts Among Us

Shelley's story from www.ghosts.org/stories/test/viewstory.php?sid=1231& PHPSESSID=5e83070034b4fd1a8432537f062cf2

Virginia's story from *Man, Myth, & Magic,* "Poltergeist" entry.

Poltergeist research and Resch hoax from www.skepdic.com/poltergeist/ and James Randi, *An Encyclopedia of Frauds, Claims, and Hoaxes of the Occult and Supernatural.*

Chapter 2: A History of Hauntings

Mesopotamian ghosts from Jo Ann Scurlock, "Death and the Afterlife in Ancient Mesopotamian Thought," in Jack M. Sasson, ed., *Civilizations of the Ancient Near East,* vol. 3 (New York: Scribner's, 1995), 1883–1893.

Ghosts and the media from "Never Seen a Ghost? Then TV May Be Your Teacher," *Purdue News,* October 17, 1997, www.news.uns.purdue.edu/html4ever/1997/ 971017.Sparks.survey/ and Matthew Nisbet, "Cultural Indicators of the Paranormal: Tracking the Media/Belief Nexus," CSICOP Science and the Media, March 22, 2006, www.csicop.org/scienceandmedia/indicators

Chapter 3: What Do Ghosts Want?

Richard Senate quote and Kirsten's story from "They See Dead People!" *People* 64, issue 19 (Nov. 7, 2005): 91–92.

Malagasy ghosts from Peter Tyson, "Legends of Madagascar," *NOVA: Secrets of the Crocodile Caves,* www.pbs.org/wgbh/nova/croccaves/legends

Donne from *Man, Myth, & Magic,* "Ghost" entry.

Greenbrier ghost from www.paranormal.about.com/library/weekly/aa020501a/ and the Greenbrier Ghost page of Ferrum College's online collection of West Virginia's music and literature, www.ferrum.edu/AppLit/StudyG/west/htm/ grghost/ and "Can the Dead Return from the Grave?" *Monroe Watchman,* December 16, 1971, published online by the West Virginia Division of Culture and History at www.wvculture/org/history/notewv/ ghost1/

Chapter 4: Spectral Sites

Borley Rectory and Harry Price from *Man, Myth, & Magic* and *Britannia Internet Magazine*, www.britannia.com/history/legend/borley/ and *Foxearth and District Local History Society*, www.foxearth.org.uk/TheHauntedRectory/ and www.prairieghosts.com/brectory/ and www.prairieghosts.com/spr/ and www.harryprice.co.uk

Cock Lane haunting from Ronald C. Finucane, *Ghosts: Appearances of the Dead and Cultural Transformation*.

Whaley House from www.whaleyhouse.org/haunted

Nickell case from Larry Weinstein, "The Visit," *Skeptical Briefs* newsletter, June 2001, www.csicop.org/sb/2001-06/visit

Singapore subway stations from www.haunted-places.com/International

Lighthouse legends from www.paranormal.about.com/library/weekly/aa032601a

Delta Queen from V. Fred Rayser, "Ghosts of the Mississippi River," *Fate*, October 1, 2000.

Lady Lovibond from www.everything2.com/index.pl?node_id=1338771

Amityville from Joe Nickell, "Amityville: The Horror of It All," *Skeptical Inquirer*, January/February 2003, www.csicop.org/si/2003-01/amityville

Chapter 5: Spirit Rappers and Toe Crackers

Defoe from Ronald C. Finucane, *Ghosts: Appearances of the Dead and Cultural Transformation*.

Fox sisters from Ruth Brandon, *The Spiritualists* and Barbara Weisberg, *Talking to the Dead*.

Spiritualist movement and Spiritualist National Union from Brandon, *The Spiritualists*; Weisberg, *Talking to the Dead*; multiple entries in *Man, Myth, & Magic*; and Mary Roach, *Spook: Science Tackles the Afterlife*.

Chapter 6: Modern Mediums and Ghost Hunters

Modern mediums from Joe Nickell, "John Edward: Hustling the Bereaved," *Skeptical Inquirer*, November/December 2001, www.csicop.org/si/2001-11/i-files/ and Joe Nickell, "Investigating Spirit Communication," *Skeptical Briefs* newsletter, September 1998, www.csicop.org/sb/98-09/i-files/ and Michael Shermer, "Psychic for a Day," in *Science Friction: Where the Known Meets the*

Unknown (New York: Times Books, 2005) and Mary Roach, *Spook: Science Tackles the Afterlife.*

Spooks and scientists from Dean Radin, "Seeking Spirits in the Laboratory" and Michael Persinger and Stanley Koren, "Predicting the Characteristics of Haunt Phenomena from Geomagnetic Factors and Brain Sensitivity: Evidence from Field and Experimental Studies" in James Houran and Rense Lange, *Hauntings and Poltergeists: Multidisciplinary Perspectives*; Mary Roach, *Spook: Science Tackles the Afterlife*; "Science Wrecks a Good Ghost Story," www.torontoghosts.org/science/ and "The Ghosts of Edinburgh Castle," www.paranormal.about.com/library/weekly/aa042301a/ and Arran Frood, "Ghosts All in the Mind," BBC news online, www.news.bbc.co.uk/1/hi/sci/tech/3044607.stm

What Do You Think?

Bell Witch from www.bellwitch.org (the site of Patrick A. Fitzhugh, author of two books about the haunting) and www.mtskeptics.homestead.com/BellWitch (a critical review of the case by a member of the Middle Tennessee Skeptics).

Gallup poll from Mark Dolliver, "A Nation of Skeptics? Don't You Believe It," *Adweek* 46, issue 27 (July 11, 2005): 31.

Index

Page numbers for illustrations are in boldface.

About the Author

Rebecca Stefoff's many books for young readers cover a wide range of topics in science, history, and literature. Scary stories and vampire movies are among her favorite entertainments. As a member of CSICOP (the Committee for the Scientific Investigation of Claims of the Paranormal), Stefoff supports a thoughtful, research-based approach to supernatural subjects. She lives in Portland, Oregon, and has never seen a ghost.